Key Stage 3
Year 8 Workbook

Name: _____

Class: _____

ENGLISH

John Green

First published 1999

Reprinted 1999
Letts Educational,
9-15 Aldine Street
London W12 8AW
Tel: 020 8740 2270
Fax: 020 8740 2280

Text: © John Green 1999

Design and illustrations © BPP (Letts Educational) Ltd 1999

Design and page layout: Ken Vail Graphic Design, Cambridge

Illustrations: Sylvie Poggio Artists Agency (Rosalind Hudson, Paul McCaffrey, Phil Smith and Sarah Warburton)

British Library Cataloguing-in-Publication Data

A CIP record for this book is available from the British Library

ISBN 1 84085 216 X

Printed and Bound in Spain.

Letts Educational is the trading name of BPP (Letts Educational) Ltd

Acknowledgements

Extracts and articles reproduced by kind permission of: p1 © *Daily Mail* 1999; pp2–3 © Times Newspapers Ltd, 1999; p4 © Telegraph Group Limited, London, 1999; p8, *Jim, Who Ran Away from his Nurse and was Eaten by a Lion*, the Peters Fraser and Dunlop Group on behalf of the Estate of Hilaire Belloc; pp11–14, *A Son of the Soil*, Pearson Education Limited for William Katiyo; pp24–26 Wakefield City Centre Partnership; pp29–32, *Journey's End*, Curtis Brown Ltd, London, on behalf of the Estate of R.C. Sherriff, © the Estate of R.C. Sherriff; pp35–38, *The Life and Death of Cholmondeley*, Curtis Brown Ltd, London, on behalf of the Estate of Gerald Durrell, © Gerald Durrell

Contents

Introduction: for teachers

This is one of a series of three books, for Years 7, 8 and 9, which have been compiled to support the teaching programme in the Letts *Classbook* for Key Stage 3 English.

Each of the books is free-standing and has been designed so pupils may use it independently, as a 'workbook'. However, it is likely that this book, and the series, will prove most valuable when used in conjunction with the *Classbook* and with each unit of work introduced through classroom discussion.

The intention of the series is to provide a wider range of texts and writing tasks, that give opportunities to reinforce and extend the knowledge and communication skills established through the *Classbook*. Each book does not cover the same genres – or periods – nor attempt to cover the full range of possible genres, but over the series, teachers should find sufficient variety to enable them, in conjunction with the *Classbook*, to address the requirements of the National Curriculum programmes of study for Key Stage 3 English.

Hence, the focus in these books is on understanding and response, and writing practice. The extracts are supported by questions that encourage learning about genre characteristics. A 'twin-pronged' focus on the texts is suggested: detailed consideration of word/sentence issues, and reflection on broader matters of a whole text/genre nature. Each writing task is genre-specific and designed to reinforce the learning acquired in answering the questions, by encouraging pupils to demonstrate their understanding through practice in their own work.

It is also hoped that, over the whole series and within each book, the texts provide a good range in terms of difficulty and interest to pupils. Each teacher will need to guide pupils towards appropriate material, but the intention is that extracts should be stimulating and challenging. Within the series, the Year 7 book is intended to build a bridge between the methods and habits of working of the National Literacy Strategy at Key Stage 2 and secondary school approaches to English. The Year 8 book links with this and leads pupils towards the strategies of the Year 9 book, which is intended to point pupils forward to the work of their GCSE course at Key Stage 4.

How to use this workbook: for pupils

The format of each unit of this book is quite straightforward. You should read through the text extracts to get an idea of basic meaning and then, working with a partner, in groups, or with your teacher, discuss related issues and topics, as an introduction to the passages' subject matter. Suggested topics for discussion include 'reminders' of key words and concepts you are likely to need in developing your answers to the questions in the 'Closer reading' section. You may attempt the answers on your own, or as part of classwork.

The 'Writing practice' section is self-explanatory. For each unit there is a specific task, which focuses on the sort of writing you have just encountered in the passages you have read and discussed. Guidance is given: to help you select subject matter, to plan the organisation and structure of your writing, and to use appropriate means of expression.

The 'Follow up!' suggestions are intended to be just that – further projects you may wish to work on as an 'optional extra', or that your teacher might want to develop into a larger class project.

This book supports the work you did in the *Classbook*. The process of gradually broadening and strengthening your skills continues here, as a further selection of texts and tasks introduces you to an ever-increasing range of materials and activities.

John Green

Read these newspaper reports of the announcement of the engagement of Prince Edward to Miss Sophie Rhys-Jones.

IN BRIEF

Scheduled flight delays increase
DELAYS TO scheduled flights at London's five main airports rose from 13 to 16 minutes during the summer but charter flight delays fell to 38 minutes from 46, according to figures published by the Civil Aviation Authority yesterday.

Prince Edward to marry
PRINCE EDWARD yesterday announced his engagement to his girlfriend of five years, Sophie Rhys-Jones. The couple are hoping to marry at St George's Chapel, Windsor, in the late spring or summer.

Two more meningitis victims
A BABY GIRL and a boy, 16, died yesterday from meningitis. The eight-month-old girl died at her Birmingham home while Trevor Stockton died in hospital in Macclesfield, Cheshire. They bring to 12 the number of people known to have died from

(from The Independent, *7 January 1999)*

The Royal Romantic

By RICHARD KAY

PRINCE Edward unveiled plans yesterday for a thoroughly modern marriage.

But he displayed old-fashioned chivalry when it came to the proposal. After formally asking Sophie to be his bride, he then made a special trip to see her father Christopher to request her hand in marriage. 'He asked my permission and I was delighted,' said a beaming Mr Rhys-Jones. 'I think my daughter will do very, very well.' The couple, who have been together for nearly six years, will marry later this year. But in a break with royal convention they will continue their careers – his in television and hers in public relations after the wedding.

PR girl and her Prince

Yesterday, after posing for photos at St James's Palace, they each went back to work.

They have also chosen to reject a costly state ceremony, unlike Prince Charles and Prince Andrew. They want a low-key family wedding at St George's Chapel, Windsor.

Yesterday the couple kissed in public and showed off Sophie's engagement ring, a glittering triple diamond in a modern design, estimated by one London jeweller to have cost as much as £105,000.

Buckingham Palace declined to comment on the cost or how Edward, who receives a £96,000-a-year allowance from the Queen, was able to afford it.

The Queen and the Duke of Edinburgh were said to be thrilled at the couple's decision. At nearly 35, their youngest son is the oldest to marry.

Prince Edward proposed to Sophie just before Christmas but they agreed to keep it a secret until he had spoken to her father who lives with his wife in a £600,000 farmhouse in Kent. Asked how he proposed, the Prince joked: 'Well, I spoke it."

He went on: 'I managed to take her completely by surprise. She had no idea that it was coming, which is completely what I wanted.'

Sophie, who is 34 in two weeks time, added: 'I was slightly stunned for a minute, then I realised I should answer the question. I said, "Yes, yes please".'

Edward said: 'We are the best of friends and we happen to love each other very much.'

Pressed on why he had taken so long to pop the question, he said it was 'impossible for anyone else to understand'.

He said: 'But I don't think it would have been right before and I don't think Sophie would have said "Yes". Hopefully by the fact that she did say "Yes", I must have got the timing right.'

Sophie admitted the prospect of joining the Royal Family was 'nerve-racking'. She added: 'But I am ready for it now and I am fully aware of the responsibilities and commitments.' Prince Charles was told the news before he and Harry set off for their Swiss ski-ing holiday.

(from the Daily Mail, *7 January 1999)*

'We are the very best of friends … we love each other as well very much, and it's great'

Family wedding at Windsor for Prince Edward

By ALAN HAMILTON

PRINCE EDWARD is determined to have a family wedding rather than a public spectacle when he crowns a five-year courtship by marrying Sophie Rhys-Jones this year.

The couple, whose engagement was announced by Buckingham Palace yesterday, will marry in the late spring or early summer at St George's Chapel, spiritual home of the Order of the Garter inside Windsor Castle. The Queen and the Duke of Edinburgh were said to be thrilled at the news of their youngest son's impending marriage to the 33-year-old public relations executive.

Miss Rhys-Jones's parents – whose permission the Prince sought as well as that of his own – said at their home near Tunbridge Wells that they were equally delighted by the announcement.

Senior Palace sources insisted last night that the decision not to turn his wedding into a major tourist attraction in central London was the Prince's alone, and that he had not faced any pressure from the Queen or Downing Street to arrange a scaled-down ceremony more in keeping with the mood of Blairite Britain.

But sources acknowledged that the 34-year-old Prince was 'not unconscious' of changes in public perception of the monarchy since the last first-rank royal wedding: that of the Duke and Duchess of York in Westminster Abbey in 1986.

Posing for photographs in the garden of St James's Palace yesterday, the Prince said he had a particular fondness for Windsor, and that it was 'somewhere slightly different'. Miss Rhys-Jones, showing off her white gold ring set with heart-shaped diamonds from Asprey & Garrard, said she expected a high degree of interest, but that the wedding was essentially a personal matter and a family occasion.

If the ceremony is low-key, it will be so only by comparison with the first marriage of his mother, aunt, brothers and sister; St George's can accommodate more than 800 guests. The Palace said last night that no decision had yet been taken on whether to allow live television coverage of the service.

Officials pointed out last night that Prince Edward, who is seventh in line to the throne, was a much less high-profile figure than the Prince of Wales; he has followed his own career and performed relatively few public engagements. Like most other members of his family, he is not supported by the Civil List.

Genealogists suggested that on his marriage, Prince Edward may be created Duke of Cambridge, although, in line with present-day trends, it may be a lifetime dukedom rather than an hereditary one.

Speculation has surrounded the couple since they first met at a real tennis match in 1993, launching one of the longest unofficial courtships in modern royal history. At the time, the monarchy was at a low point, with the Princess Royal divorced and remarried, the Prince's elder brothers both on their way to divorce.

Prince Edward has been under an enormous

obligation not to repeat his siblings' marital mistakes. By comparison with his own lengthy courtship, both the Prince of Wales and the Duke of York virtually rushed into marriage, although the Princess Royal had a longer and more leisurely courtship with Captain Mark Phillips.

Miss Rhys-Jones was adamant yesterday that she and the Prince had not lived together during their long association, but it is a fine definition. A suite of rooms at Buckingham Palace was put at her disposal early in the courtship, and she has used them frequently.

She has also been a regular companion of the Prince at Royal Family gatherings, including the annual summer holiday at Balmoral and the Christmas break at Sandringham, where for several years she has joined the Queen and other members of the family at church on Christmas Day.

The Prince and Miss Rhys-Jones are several years older than the average age for first marriage, and have had ample opportunity to get to know each other well. The Prince has been exceedingly careful in ensuring that he has picked the right partner. A successful union has great potential to restore the monarchy's standing; another failure would be a dangerously damaging blow to public perception of the institution.

He acknowledged as much yesterday when he said: 'We are the very best of friends, and that's essential. It also helps that we happen to love each other as well very much, and it's great. We are very happy at the moment, and long may it continue.'

The Prince finally proposed to Miss Rhys-Jones shortly before Christmas, putting an end to an agonisingly long wait. Apart from a natural caution engendered by the marital fate of his siblings, he was keen to wait until anniversary mourning for the death of Diana, Princess of Wales, was well past.

Both parties were also anxious to put their professional careers on a sound footing. The Prince has spent several years building up his television company, Ardent Productions, making several documentaries on royal history and therefore well aware of the potential for good or harm for the monarchy's future that lies in his hands. Miss Rhys-Jones is now a partner in a successful London public relations consultancy.

Both said yesterday that they intended to continue working. They plan to live relatively modestly at Bagshot Park, the house in Surrey leased by Prince Edward last year.

Congratulations flowed in as soon as the news became public. A spokesman for the Prime Minister, who was told before he left the Seychelles for an official visit to South Africa, said that both Tony and Cherie Blair were delighted. William Hague and Paddy Ashdown also sent their good wishes, as did Dr George Carey and Cardinal Basil Hume.

COURT CIRCULAR

SANDRINGHAM HOUSE January 6: It is with the greatest pleasure that The Queen and The Duke of Edinburgh announce the betrothal of their beloved son The Prince Edward to Miss Sophie Rhys-Jones, daughter of Mr and Mrs Christopher Rhys-Jones.

The official announcement in *The Times* Court Circular.

(from *The Times*, 7 January 1999)

We are the best of friends

Prince Edward to wed Sophie after five-year courtship

By Robert Hardman

THE longest royal courtship of modern times reached a happy conclusion yesterday with the announcement that Prince Edward is to marry Sophie Rhys-Jones, his girlfriend for more than five years. 'We are very happy at the moment and long may it continue,' he said.

The couple plan to marry in the spring or early summer at St George's Chapel, Windsor.

There will be none of the pageantry and pomp of other royal weddings, however. It is to be a family wedding rather than a state occasion.

The Queen and Prince Philip and Miss Rhys-Jones's parents, Christopher and Mary, were said to be 'thrilled and delighted'.

It is not known whether the Prince will be offered – or will accept – the customary dukedom conferred on the sons of sovereigns. For the moment, Miss Rhys-Jones is due to become HRH The Princess Edward.

The Prince, 34, who runs his own television production company, and Miss Rhys-Jones, 33, a public relations consultant, appeared in the garden of St James's Palace for the world's media.

There the Prince disclosed that he had proposed before Christmas. The couple had then kept the news a secret until the Prince could ask Miss Rhys-Jones's father for his daughter's hand.

Despite the length of their romance, the proposal came out of the blue.

'I managed to take her completely by surprise,' the Prince said. Her response after a stunned pause was: 'Yes. Yes, please.'

After their wedding, the couple will live at Bagshot Park, a Victorian mansion in Surrey which the Prince has leased from the Crown Estate. He will retain his private apartment and office at Buckingham Palace, while Miss Rhys-Jones is likely to give up the separate room she has there.

The Prince and Miss Rhys-Jones met during the summer of 1993 at a charity real tennis match which he was organising and she was promoting. Since then Miss Rhys-Jones has been a regular guest at the most private of Royal Family events and is well aware of what to expect.

Asked why he had taken so long to pop the question, the Prince said: 'It's impossible for anyone else to understand why, but I don't think it would have been right before and I don't think that Sophie would have said yes. Hopefully, by the fact that she did say yes, I must have got the timing right.'

Requests that he kiss the bride-to-be were rewarded with one peck on the cheek – quite a concession for a man who has always refused to parade his relationships in public.

'The trouble is, everybody always speculating always made it very difficult,' he said. 'Every time there was another round of speculation, I had to go very quiet again.'

Miss Rhys-Jones decided to clear up some misconceptions, particularly those surrounding her private room at the Palace.

'Contrary to popular opinion, we have never lived together,' she said, 'and I have never issued any ultimatums.'

She wore a ring of three diamonds in a modern setting from the royal jewellers, Asprey & Garrard.

St George's Chapel would be 'a wonderful setting' for the wedding, the Prince said.

Their hopes of keeping the occasion as private as possible might make him 'deeply unpopular', he joked.

While there will be public glimpses of the occasion, there is unlikely to be live television coverage.

For the moment, Miss Rhys-Jones intends to continue her work as chairman of the public relations company, RJ-H, of which she is a co-owner.

The couple received many messages of congratulation after the announcement, including one from the Prime Minister. Other party leaders and the Archbishops of Canterbury and Westminster were among the well-wishers.

Other members of the Royal Family refrained from making public comments because no one wanted to upstage the Prince.

(from *The Daily Telegraph*, 7 January 1999)

Talk about

- Why do you think people read newspapers? Why do you think there are so many different papers? Why do people choose one paper rather than another?

- What are the most important things readers need to know when an engagement or any other sort of public announcement is made?

- In what ways do newspapers set out stories differently from books and other forms of printed material?

- What do these words mean?
engagement betrothal wedding marriage headlines sub-headings column inches lay-out journalist reporter verb stem suffix

Closer reading

Word and sentence work

1 Look at the main headline for each report.
- In what ways does each give emphasis to a different aspect of the report?

2 The opening sentence in the reports in *The Independent* and the *Daily Mail* is only about half as long as the opening sentence in the reports in *The Times* and *The Daily Telegraph*.
- What differences are there in the impact of these opening sentences and the effect they have on the reader?

3 Explain the effect of each of these phrases from the opening sentence in each report:

'…announced his engagement…'
(*The Independent*)

'…reached a happy conclusion…'
(*The Daily Telegraph*)

'…is determined to have a family wedding rather than a public spectacle…'
(*The Times*).

4 The word 'courtship' is formed from the verb stem 'court' and a suffix '–ship'.
- What effect does this suffix usually have on the meaning of the word it is added to?
- List five other examples of words ending in '–ship', with their meanings.

5 Explain the significance of the phrase 'a thoroughly modern marriage' in the *Daily Mail* report.
- What words in the sentence that follows that phrase apparently contradict this idea? Why?

Text and genre work

6 The report in *The Independent* is much shorter than the others and appeared on page 5. The other reports are all from the front page.
- Look at the heading for the column and the other news items included in it. What reasons do you think *The Independent* has for reporting the story in this way?

7 Why do you think *The Times* has included the insert from the 'Court Circular', usually headed with the royal coat of arms?

8 What aspect of the story is emphasised in the first paragraph of each of the reports?

● Why do you think each has been chosen?

9 What use is made of quotations/comments from people in these reports?

● Whose comments are quoted first and what other quotations are included?

● What does this suggest about the different attitudes and priorities of each newspaper?

10 Complete the following table, indicating the order in which each aspect of the story is dealt with in each report.

● Put a cross where a report doesn't mention one of the points, and write any other points in the final row.

● Use the information you have gathered to write an account of the differences between the four reports, explaining how each attempts to appeal to its readers in its own way.

Aspect of story	The Independent	The Daily Mail	The Daily Telegraph	The Times
When and where the wedding might take place				
Possible style of wedding				
The engagement ring				
Parents' attitude towards the engagement				
Possible titles and home				
Nature of their relationship				
Their attitude to future roles/work				
Public attitudes towards the royal family				
Any other points				

Writing practice: special occasion

Write two reports – as though for different newspapers – of an important public announcement.

- You do not have to include real people. For example, you could write about the on-screen engagement of two television soap opera stars.

- You don't have to write about an engagement or wedding. For example, your subject could be the return to Earth of the first humans to visit another planet.

- Concentrate on organising your material for the two reports in different ways and choosing appropriate vocabulary, to make them appeal to different groups of people.

- You could specify, for example, that one is a report for parents, teachers or adults generally, and the other for teenagers, younger children, or whomever – depending on the subject you choose.

- You might like to use this frame to plan your writing.

Subject		
Ideas	**First report**	**Second report**
Main points of story: ● time ● place ● people, etc.	Sequence of points/paragraphs	Sequence of points/paragraphs
Headlines	e.g. Incredible!	e.g. Amazing new…announced
Quotations	e.g. 'Lucky me,' said…	e.g. 'I have been so lucky,' declared…
Opening sentence	e.g. 'The world is a different place this morning.'	e.g. Yesterday's announcement that …has implications for the whole of mankind, as never again will…

Follow up!

Organise a survey to discover which newspapers your classmates, their families and your teachers read.

- Ask why they choose a particular paper. What do they find especially interesting? What do they like/dislike?

Classbook reference
Unit 19,
page 216

Eaten by a lion

Read this poem by Hilaire Belloc. It tells the sad story of Jim and warns all children of what can go wrong if they do not heed the warnings and advice of adults!

Jim, Who Ran Away from his Nurse, and was Eaten by a Lion

There was a boy whose name was Jim;
His parents were very good to him.
They gave him tea, and cakes, and jam,
And slices of delicious ham,
5 And chocolate with pink inside,
And little tricycles to ride,
And read him stories through and through,
And even took him to the Zoo –
But there it was the dreadful fate
10 Befell him, which I now relate.

You know – at least you *ought* to know,
For I have often told you so –
That children never are allowed
To leave their nurses in a crowd;
15 Now this was Jim's especial foible,
He ran away when he was able,
And on this inauspicious day
He slipped his hand and ran away!
He hadn't gone a yard when – Bang!
20 With open jaws, a lion sprang,
And hungrily began to eat
The boy: beginning at his feet.

Now, just imagine how it feels
When first your toes and then your heels,
25 And then by gradual degrees,
Your shins and ankles, calves and knees,
Are slowly eaten, bit by bit.
No wonder Jim detested it!
No wonder that he shouted 'Hi!'
30 The honest keeper heard his cry,
Though very fat he almost ran
To help the little gentleman.
'Ponto!' he ordered as he came,
(For Ponto was the lion's name),
35 'Ponto!' he cried, with angry frown,
'Let go, Sir! Down, Sir! Put it down!'

The lion made a sudden stop,
He let the dainty morsel drop,
And slunk reluctant to his cage,
40 Snarling with disappointed rage.
But when he bent him over Jim,
The honest keeper's eyes were dim.
The lion having reached his head,
The miserable boy was dead!

45 When Nurse informed his parents, they
Were more concerned than I can say:
His Mother, as she dried her eyes,
Said, 'Well – it gives me no surprise,
He would not do as he was told!'
50 His Father, who was self-controlled,
Bade all his children round attend
To James's miserable end,
And always keep a-hold of Nurse
For fear of finding something worse.

Hilaire Belloc

Talk about

- What sort of world is suggested by 'tea, and cakes, and jam' and 'nurses' in this poem?

- Discuss any visits to zoos you have made.

- Have you ever disobeyed an adult, with disastrous consequences? – not simply being punished. Describe it.

- What are the differences between **fairy stories, fables, cautionary tales, parables, myths** and **legends**?

- What do these words mean?

  narrator   moral   rhyme   word stem

Closer reading

Word and sentence work

1 What phrase does the writer use to begin the poem to suggest it's 'only a story'?

2 Look at the word 'stories' in line 7. This is the plural form of 'story'.

- How has the plural been formed?

- What would be the plural form of 'monkey'?

- Write down the rule that governs the formation of plurals from words ending in '–y'.

3 What is the effect of the dash – after 'Zoo', at the end of line 8?

4 How does the writer emphasise the effect of the word 'Bang' (line 19)?

- In the third verse how does he show the way the keeper spoke to the lion?

5 'Slipped' in line 18 and 'beginning' in line 22 are both word stems with a suffix added.

- What effect has the adding of the suffixes '–ed' and '–ing' had on the spelling of the word stem?

- Why hasn't this happened with 'informed' and 'finding' in the last verse (lines 45 and 54 respectively)?

Text and genre work

6 Do you think Jim was spoilt as a child?

7 The writer says that Jim was 'slowly eaten' (line 27). In what other way does he suggest that being eaten was a slow process?

8 Look at the beginning of the fourth verse (line 37). How does the sound of the words support the meaning at this point?

9 Explain the rhyming pattern of this poem.

- What effect does it have on the poem's general tone and mood?

10 The last two lines of the poem contain 'the moral' of this cautionary tale.

- How has the writer prepared the reader earlier for the lesson that has to be learned?

Writing practice: a warning to naughty children

Write your own cautionary tale about a child who does something wrong and suffers dire consequences.

● Use the same verse form as Hilaire Belloc, trying to maintain a regular rhyming pattern.

● Use the framework below, or try a version of your own.

> *Poor Sad* _____
>
> There was a _____ whose name was _____ ;
>
> _____ .
>
> They gave _____ ,
>
> And _____ ,
>
> And _____ .
>
> But then occurred such dreadful pain
>
> That _____ would never _____ again.
>
> Now _____ would never _____ as _____ should,
>
> So none ever called _____ good.
>
> And so, one day _____ ,
>
> _____ .

Follow up!

Listen to a recording of, or read, Stanley Holloway's monologue *Albert and the Lion*.

● In what ways is this story similar to Hilaire Belloc's?

● Why is it more amusing when heard/read aloud?

● Prepare a reading for your class of Hilaire Belloc's poem about Jim.

Classbook reference

Unit 15, page 158

Read this extract from Wilson Katiyo's novel *A Son of the Soil*. This story, first published in 1976, tells of some of the stresses and struggles of a black boy growing up in colonial Zimbabwe. Young Alexio is forced to leave the village where he was born and live and work with a member of his extended family, Rudo. Inevitably, not all his experiences are happy ones.

By the time Alexio arrived in Salisbury, Rudo was an expert in every aspect of her job. She could now speak English. Madam had been kind enough to allow Rudo to have Alexio live at the yard on condition he did not interfere with Rudo's work too much.

On the day Alexio was to arrive, Madam gave Rudo time to go and meet him. Rudo was allowed to use Madam's bicycle. When Rudo arrived with Alexio sitting on the bicycle carrier, the first thing she had to do was make him look presentable.

She wiped his face and hair with a damp cloth and dressed him in one of her blouses, a white one, which Madam had given her. Leading the boy by the hand, she then took him to be 'seen' by Madam. They entered the house by the back door and waited for Madam in the kitchen. Soon, Madam walked in.

'This is the child, Madam,' reported Rudo in her usual soft-spoken voice.

'Oh! He is quite a man. Now Rudo, if you can't do your work because of him, he will have to go. Do you understand?'

'Yes, Madam.'

'How old is he?'

'I don't know, Madam.'

'What's his name?'

'Alexio, Madam.'

'Funny name – never mind. Do you think he might fit into some of Peter's or John's clothes? I should think he will. Let me go and see what I can dig up.'

Madam disappeared into Master Peter and Master John's rooms. When she came back, she gave Rudo three pairs of short trousers, two shirts and a sweater for Alexio. From somewhere Master Peter and Master John raced into the house and into the kitchen.

They saw Alexio.

'Hello!' 'Hello!'

'What's your name?'

'Have you come to live with Rudo?'

'Come, I will show you my room and my toys.'

'I am John.'

'I am Peter and – and I have more toys than John!'

It was hard to tell what Alexio was feeling or thinking. His mature face remained expressionless. He looked unaffected and remained the same throughout.

'Can I feel your hair?' asked Master Peter and proceeded to put his hand on Alexio's head. Alexio forcefully warded off Master Peter's hand.

'That's enough, boys,' said Madam, who had been watching the scene, 'come Peter, John. Back to your rooms! … I said out! Can't you see you are frightening the poor creature!'

The two white boys walked out of the kitchen. Alexio thought Madam was shouting at him. He clung to Rudo's legs.

'All right, Rudo. But please try not to bring him in the house too much. He causes the boys too much excitement.'

'Yes, Madam. Thank you, Madam.'

Rudo taught Alexio never to go to the house unless she called him. This proved to be very easy as Alexio was used to being by himself. He spent most of his time in front of the shack. He liked drawing all sorts of pictures on sand. At first he used to draw whole

villages, people and animals. But in time, he began drawing things he saw around him – cars, bicycles and white people. When Rudo gave him a toy car, he used to spend hours building roads, moulding mountains out of sand and pretending to travel from one village to another. Sometimes Rudo used to take him along when she took Master Peter and Master John to the park or to the playground. But of course Rudo could not let him play with Master John, Master Peter and the other white children. It was not allowed. Alexio usually sat with Rudo and the other black nannies who also brought children to the park or to the playground.

Madam told her children not to play with Alexio as they frightened him. She also pointed out that Alexio couldn't speak

English so the children wouldn't understand him anyway. Madam instructed Rudo never to allow the children to play with Alexio as there was a danger that a fight could occur. But Master Peter and Master John used to sneak out of the house and go to the shack to play with Alexio. Rudo knew about this but she used to turn a blind eye. She pretended to be angry when she had to 'discover' them and bring play to an end.

Gradually, the children got used to playing together. On the whole, they got on very well. Now and again, however, some minor fights broke out. Rudo always managed to stop the fights before anyone got hurt. These fights were easily mutually concealed from Madam. The children from neighbouring houses also used to secretly come and play. Play had to be centred outside the shack as Alexio refused to go anywhere else. Although language was a problem, the children somehow managed to communicate. As time passed, Alexio began to speak some English. Rudo was very pleased by this development. Life went on very much like this for about two years.

Then one day, Master Peter and Master John came from school and went to play with Alexio. They found Alexio asleep on the sand outside Rudo's shack. He did this quite often, especially on hot afternoons. Master John and Master Peter had with them their latest toys – water pistols. They woke Alexio up by squirting water on his face. When Alexio woke up, he grabbed Master Peter and took his water pistol from him. He squirted water on Master Peter's face. Somehow, this annoyed Master Peter very much. Master Peter demanded his water pistol back. Alexio handed it over. Then Master John squirted water into Alexio's face. Again Alexio did what he had done with Master Peter. But when Master John demanded his

pistol back, Alexio refused to hand it back. He said he didn't want to play that game. Master Peter supported his brother's demand for the pistol. Alexio still refused to hand it over. The two white boys attacked him. The fight was mainly between Alexio and Master Peter. After rolling over each other several times and scratching each other, Alexio gained advantage over Master Peter. He sat on Master Peter's tummy and went on hitting him on the face. Both children were screaming and covered in blood. Unfortunately, Rudo, who usually stopped these fights, had gone out to the shops. Master John, after standing about helplessly for some minutes, tried to pull Alexio off Master Peter. He had asked for it. Alexio went for Master John and soon had him on the floor. But Master Peter stood up and saw a heavy plank just outside Rudo's shack. With it, he began pounding Alexio. Alexio went for the plank. It was while the struggle for the plank was going on that the Mrs from next door, who had heard the screams, arrived and stopped the fight. For some reason her immediate reaction was to slap Alexio several times. Just then, Rudo arrived. Again, like the Mrs, Rudo's immediate reaction was to beat Alexio. Frantically, she hit the boy until he couldn't cry any more.

She and the Mrs took Master Peter and Master John inside the house. They cleaned up the children and treated their scratches. There was no question of hiding this fight from Madam, Rudo knew. Was she going to lose her job? When Madam came home, she was shocked by the state of her children. Shivering with fear, Rudo reported the little she knew about the fight to Madam.

'I could send you to jail for this, you know! I have always known there was something sinister about that little bastard! Get the bicycle and take him away from here! Don't let me ever see him again! Come on! Out!'

Rudo went out. Madam telephoned the doctor. Alexio was still lying where he had fallen after Rudo beat him. He wasn't crying. He lay very still. Rudo walked past him and disappeared inside the shack. When she came out, she had a cloth bag in which she had thrown the few things that belonged to Alexio.

Talk about

- How are words used to convey attitudes and prejudices? Consider the implications of these statements: 'She's prejudiced; you have your own opinions; I'm open-minded.'

- Discuss examples of prejudiced behaviour that you have come across.

- At what point does the reader begin to feel that a crisis is bound to happen?

- What do these words mean?

  prejudice attitude bias bigotry

Closer reading

Word and sentence work

1 Why is Rudo's employer known as 'Madam' and her sons as 'Master Peter' and 'Master John'?

● What other words and phrases in the first two paragraphs of this extract show that Madam has complete authority over Rudo?

2 Alexio was allowed to 'live at the yard'. He was 'taught...never to go to the house unless she (Rudo) called him'. 'He spent most of his time in front of the shack.'

● What do these quotations suggest about the way Alexio was regarded?

3 Look at the conversation between Madam, her sons, Rudo and Alexio.

● What impression does this give of the attitudes the characters have towards each other ?

● What words and phrases give you these impressions? You may answer by completing this table:

Character	Attitude	Words and phrases
Madam attitude towards → Rudo / Alexio / Her sons		
Rudo attitude towards → Madam		
Alexio attitude towards → Madam / The boys / Rudo		
Peter and John attitude towards → Madam / Alexio		

4 Look again at this section of conversation.

● What do you notice about the sentence structures used?

● How far do you think this supports the points you have made about the different characters' attitudes in your answer to question 3?

5 The final paragraph in this extract contains mainly short sentences. Why do you think this is and what effect do you think they have?

Text and genre work

6 Alexio spends most of his time playing. What does he do?

7 Why was Alexio not allowed to play with Master Peter and Master John and the other white children?

- What reasons are given?
- How true do these reasons seem?

8 How does the fight start and why does it get so fierce?

9 Look at the three short paragraphs leading up to the long paragraph that describes the big fight between the boys. Think about what information each paragraph gives and how they link with each other.

- How do these three paragraphs prepare the reader for the events that follow?

10 Why do both 'the Mrs from next door' and Rudo immediately hit Alexio?

Writing practice: a victim of unfair treatment or prejudice

Write a story in which prejudice is the central theme. It may be based on events you have seen or heard about and involve people you know either yourself or through friends, or it may be an entirely imagined story.

Think about:

- what form prejudice is going to take in the story
- what characters will be involved and how they will behave
- what events will happen to bring out the prejudice and your characters' reactions
- how your story will develop
  - in strict order of events as they happen
  - in flashback
  - an 'historic' account after it's all over
- who will relate the story
  - the central character/someone involved (first person)
  - someone watching (third person)
- an effective opening and ending for your story.

Follow up!

There is much reference today to **politically correct language**. For example, in years gone by, comments might be given by an appropriate 'spokesman'; today the term is usually 'spokesperson'. Previously, a meeting might have been run by 'the Chairman', addressed either as 'Mister Chairman' or 'Madam Chairman'; today, the term is likely to be just 'the Chair'.

- Make a list of words you believe contain prejudice and give your replacement terms, explaining why they would be preferable. For example, consider the word 'craftsman'.

Classbook reference
Unit 13, page 131

Here are two pieces of writing about the escape of the future King Charles II after the Battle of Worcester. The first extract is written as a first-hand account soon after the event. The second passage is taken from Arthur Bryant's history of the England of King Charles II, published in 1934.

Extract A

Before his Majesty was come to Barbons bridge about half a mile out of Worcester he made several stands, and faced about, and desired the Duke of Buckingham, Lord Wilmot and others of his Commanders that they might Rally and try once more the Fortune of War, but at the Bridge consultation being held, it was concluded that the day was irrecoverably lost, and all that was now to do, was to save his Majesty from the Rebels; whereupon by the advice of his Council his Majesty resolves for Scotland; immediately after the result, one Walker of Lord Talbot's Troop was called for (who was formerly scout master to Col. Sands) to be their Guide, but being come to Kinver Heath, and day light being gone, Walker

was at a puzzle in the way; here his Majesty made a stand and consulted with the Duke of Buckingham, Earl of Derby, Lord Wilmot and others, where he might march and take some rest; the Earl of Derby told his Majesty that there was a great convenience of concealment at Boscobell house and a right honest man that kept it; his Majesty therefore resolved to go thither. The Lord Talbot being acquainted with his resolution and finding Walker dubious of the way, called for Mr. Charles Giffard to conduct his Majesty towards Boscobell, which he willingly undertakes, and being come near Sturbridge, it was a debate whether his Majesty should march through the Town or no, and resolved that all about his person should speak French.

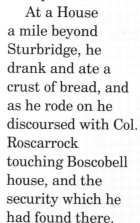

At a House a mile beyond Sturbridge, he drank and ate a crust of bread, and as he rode on he discoursed with Col. Roscarrock touching Boscobell house, and the security which he had found there.

Upon further consideration by his Majesty and Council, and to the end that the company might not know whether his Majesty directly intended; Mr. Giffard was desired to conduct his Majesty to some house near Boscobell, the better to blind the design of going thither. Mr. Giffard proposed

White-ladies lying about half a mile beyond Boscobell, and 26 miles from Worcester.

His Majesty and his Retinue being safely conducted to White-ladies by Mr. Giffard, alighted, now as they hoped out of danger of any surprise by pursuit, George Pendrill opened the Dores, and after his Majesty and his Lords were entered the House, his Majesty's Horse was brought into the Hall, and by this time it was about break of day; here was every one in a sad consult how to escape the Fury of the Rebels, but the greatest care was to save the King.

Whilst Rich. and Will. were thus sent for, his Majesty had been advised to rub his hands on the back of the chimney, and with them his Face for a Disguise, and some person had disorderly cut of his Locks; his Majesty (having put off his Princely Ornaments, distributed his Gold among his Servants), put on a coarse Shirt borrowed of Edw. Martin, who lived in the House, and Rich. Pendrill's Green Suit and leather Doublet, but both Rich. and Will. adviseth the company to haste away, in regard there was a Troop of Rebels quartered but Three miles distant.

R. Pendrell conducted his Majesty out at a back dore (unknown to most of the company), and carried him into an Adjacent Wood called Spring Coppice belonging to Boscobell about half a mile from White-ladies, Will., Hump. and George scouring abroad and bringing what news they could learn to his Majesty in the Wood.

By that time R. Pendrell had conveyed his Majesty into the obscurest part of the Coppice it was about Sun Rising on Thursday morning and it rained very fast, in so much that the thickest Tree in the Wood was not able to keep his Majesty dry, nor was there any thing for him to sit on, therefore Richard went and borrowed a Blanket of Francis Yates, which he folded and laid on the ground under a Tree for his Majesty to sit on.

At the same time that Richard borrowed the blanket, he spake to Goodwife Yates to bring some victuals into the Wood at a place he appointed her; she presently made ready a messe of milk, and some Butter and Eggs, and brought them to his Majesty, who being some what surprised to see a Woman, said cheerfully to her, 'Good Woman, can you be faithful to a distressed Cavalier?' She answered, 'Yes, Sir, I will Dye rather than discover you.'

Extract B

At Barbourne Bridge, where the grass highway to the north was crowded with flying men, there had been a hasty consultation. The King himself had wished to ride alone to London, trusting to arrive before news of the battle and so take ship to France. But the day was already waning, and his companions had dissuaded him from this desperate course. Leaving the main line of fugitives to the west, they rode with him across a land of wooded valleys and little hills, until at nightfall they reached Kinver Heath. Here the scout, who was leading, admitted that he was lost.

In the confusion that followed, the Earl of Derby brought forward a Catholic gentleman, Charles Giffard, owner of a remote house in Shropshire, near which he had found shelter a few days before. To Giffard and his servant, Yates, a poor rustic skilful in the ways of that country, the fugitives entrusted themselves. So guided, they came down into the hidden lands below. As complete darkness fell, romance spread her cloak over the King and hid him from the thousand eyes that sought him.

Nobody suspected the little party of Cavaliers, who walked their horses through the streets of sleeping Stourbridge. At an inn near Wordsley the King stopped for a hasty tankard of ale: then rode on through the night, a crust of bread in one hand and meat in the other. Giffard rode at his side, telling him of the secret hiding-places of Whiteladies and Boscobel, while the broken lords and officers trotted behind. For some hours they followed a maze of winding lanes, till they came to the edge of Brewood Forest. Here, fifty miles from the battlefield, and a little before dawn, the tired King saw the dark outlines of the ruined monastery of Whiteladies.

The clatter of hooves and the whispered calls of Giffard brought down the Penderels, the poor Catholic woodcutters who tenanted the house. To these humble folk the great personages, crowding into the hall, turned for help and advice. While a hasty message was sent to bring William, the eldest of the five Penderel brothers, from Boscobel, the King, in an inner chamber, broke his fast on sack and biscuits. A few minutes later Lord Derby brought in William and Richard Penderel to him, telling them that they must have a care of him and preserve him. To this they proudly and gladly assented. Richard went out to fetch some country clothes, while the King stripped and put on a rough noggen shirt. The first lines of dawn were appearing when Richard returned with an old sweaty leather doublet, a green, threadbare coat, and a greasy steeple hat without band or lining. Lord Wilmot, the stoutest and merriest of the fugitives, began to cut the royal locks with a knife, but did the job so badly that Richard was commanded to finish it, which he did in great pride with a basin and a pair of shears.

Placing his hands up the chimney, Charles, who, despite peril and weariness, could not refrain from laughing, completed his make-up by blacking his face. Then, while his companions rode off to join the flying Scots, he went out into the dawn with Richard Penderel and a billhook.

It was raining. All day the King crouched in the damp undergrowth of a little wood, called Spring Coppice. About midday Penderel's sister-in-law, Elizabeth Yates, brought him a blanket to sit on and a mess of milk, butter, and eggs. She told him news of the world outside the woods – of long streams of Scottish fugitives and pursuing Roundheads and of search-parties already at Whiteladies.

Afterwards he fell into a broken slumber.

Talk about

- Both these extracts deal with events that are loosely related to what became known as Oak-apple Day.

Check in an encyclopedia, on CD-ROM or the Internet for more information and discuss the origins of Oak-apple Day. How and why was it celebrated?

- What is the attitude of each writer towards the events described? Why is each giving an account of these events?

- What sort of book do you think each of these extracts is taken from? What features of the extracts make you think that?

- In what ways has the use of language changed between the writing of these two passages? And between then and now?

- What do these words mean?
  narrator
  personal narrative
  first-person narrative
  historical account
  outmoded expressions
  Standard English
  prefix

Closer reading

Word and sentence work

1 In Extract A, why are the names 'Rich.' and 'Will.' followed by full stops?

2 In Extract A, the writer uses phrases like 'at a puzzle in the way' and 'dubious of the way'. These are rather old-fashioned phrases.

- How would these ideas be expressed today?

- Find five other old-fashioned words or phrases in the passage and give their modern equivalent.

3 In Extract B, the writer says the companions of the King 'dissuaded him...' This word belongs to the same family as the more familiar word 'persuade'.

- What effect does the prefix 'dis–' have on meaning when added to a word stem?

- Give three other examples, with their meanings, of words with the prefix 'dis–'.

4 In Extract B, the writer uses the metaphor '...romance spread her cloak over the King and hid him from the thousand eyes...'.

- Explain as precisely as you can what the writer is saying and what effect he is trying to achieve with these words.

5 Some of the same people and places are described differently in each extract. For example, 'Mr. Charles Giffard' and '... a Catholic gentleman, Charles Giffard...'; and references to 'his Majesty' and 'the King'.

- What impressions do these different words and phrases give of the people and places they refer to?

Text and genre work

6 Complete this table, showing who, according to each extract, was with the King at the places listed. What happened there?

	Extract A		Extract B	
	People?	What happened?	People?	What happened?
Place				
Barbons/Barbourne Bridge				
Kinver Heath				
Stourbridge				
Whiteladies				
Spring Coppice				

7 How is the King disguised? Pick out the main features that are mentioned in both extracts.

8 Look carefully at the words and phrases each writer uses to describe how the King was disguised. For example, in Extract A, 'disorderly cut of his locks'.

● How do these suggest that being disguised may not have been a pleasant experience?

9 Find two places in Extract A where it gives more detail than Extract B of what took place. Why do you think this is?

10 Consider all the differences between these two extracts. Then explain what you think each writer set out to do and the effect they wished to have on the reader.

You should think about:
● each writer's choice of detail
● the way people and events are described
● each writer's portrayal of the King's character.

Writing practice: a journey to remember/forget

Sometimes making a journey – even a short one into town – can be an exciting or unusual experience. At other times, it can be boring, frightening or utterly dreadful.

Choose one such experience – pleasant or unpleasant – and write an account of it from two different points of view: your own personal standpoint and from the perspective of someone looking back and recounting the events – as history – later on.

- Each point of view will be different. The things that seem important may be different in each account.

- One account could be your brief, bad-tempered summary of events for a friend at school, or your mother's enthusiastic account to a neighbour. The other could be a chapter for a book of fascinating or unusual journeys.

- You need not include the whole journey, but try to emphasise the personal perspective on what happens in your first piece and adopt a more distant, objective approach in the second.

- You could use this frame to help plan your writing.

Possible content	First-person account	Third-person account
How will you begin your piece of writing so you clearly indicate your position as narrator?	e.g. 'My family/friends…'	e.g. 'The road from Walsall to Wolverhampton does not at first sound an appealing prospect, but…'
To what extent will you include your personal thoughts and feelings when you describe what you see and what happens?	e.g. 'I was amazed when…' 'We were so upset to see…'	e.g. 'Initially, things went smoothly…'
How will your choice of pronouns and verb forms be affected by the way you write the account?	e.g. 'I/we…' (mainly active voice?) 'We stopped…' (mainly imperfect/ simple past tenses?)	e.g. 'It…' (mainly passive voice?) 'The car had been halted by…' (mainly historic past tenses?)
How will you end your account?	e.g. 'Never again will I…'	e.g. 'The adventure drew to a close…'

Follow up!

Check in the calendar for other dates that have been traditionally celebrated in England, e.g. Shrove Tuesday, Ash Wednesday, May Day, Michaelmas, Lady Day, Hallowe'en and Advent.

- When are these days? What do they celebrate?

- How are they celebrated?

- Which additional days – like Ramadan, the Chinese New Year or the Notting Hill Carnival – should be added to the list of celebrations, to take account of the multi-cultural nature of modern society?

- Give reasons for those you suggest.

Classbook reference
Unit 20, page 228

Read this leaflet advertising a special event, the Wakefield Motoring Spectacular.

HERE IN WAKEFIELD, WE HAVE THE **'WINNING FORMULA'** FOR 3 DAYS OF SPECTACULAR FUN & **'FREE'** ENTERTAINMENT FOR ALL THE FAMILY

Everything from historic vehicle rally, displays and parades, to the latest in hi-tech vehicle design will be on show.

You can also have hands on experience when the Police, Fire Service, Army, RAF, and Cadets show off their mobile units, exhibitions/displays and vehicles.

And if that's not enough for every member of the family-Midland Bank will unveil the Stewart-Ford Formula One Racing Car in the City Centre to delight the crowds over the 3 day period.

All this plus marching bands, majorettes, civic and celebrity guests, competitions, street entertainment, not forgetting the superb high street shopping, pubs, restaurants and cafes.

We've even taken care of overnight accommodation with special rates at the City Centre Chasley Hotel. Here you can relax, wine and dine, then perhaps visit the Theatre or take in the latest movie at Cineworld's Hi-Tech Multiplex Cinema. For the more energetic try out the famous 'Westgate Run' of pubs, restaurants and vibrant state of the art nightclubs.

So, if your looking for 3 days of **'FREE'** fun, activities and entertainment, why not bring all the family and friends to this year's Wakefield Motoring Spectacular.

FRIDAY 17 JULY

✳ CATHEDRAL PRECINCT,
WAKEFIELD CITY CENTRE **10.00AM**

Midland Bank unveils the Stewart-Ford Formula One Racing Car.

✳ 23rd HISTORIC COMMERCIAL VEHICLE SOCIETY
RALLY, THORNES PARK, WAKEFIELD
FRIDAY EVENING **4.00PM**

One of the largest gatherings of historic vehicles in Europe with displays and judging of around 1000 lorries, buses, vans, military vehicles, fire engines, cars, motorcycles, working engines and models.
Plus side stalls, kiddy rides, food and entertainment

✳ ACCOMMODATION - CHASLEY HOTEL, QUEEN STREET,
WAKEFIELD - FRIDAY/SATURDAY 17/18 JULY
£35 pp/pn 'Single Room' includes Full English Breakfast.
£25 pp/pn based on 2 people sharing a 'Double/Twin Room' includes Full English Breakfast.
Direct Reservations: **Tel: 01924 372111 Fax: 01924 383648**

SATURDAY 18 JULY

WAKEFIELD CITY CENTRE **10.00AM**

✳ Grand Parade of over 100 historic vehicles from Thornes Park around the City Centre.

✳ These will then be displayed in the City Centre alongside stands/displays of new vehicles by motor dealerships including Honda, Saab, Suzuki, Seat, Toyota, Nissan, Renault, Fiat, Peugeot, Rover, VW and Audi, plus the Stewart-Ford Formula One Racing Car.

✳ There will also be Army and SSAFA (Forces Charity) displays in the new Market Performance Arena plus Morris Dancers, Military Band and Gawthorpe Junior Band.

✳ Plus civic and celebrity guests, St. Swithan's Majorettes, bands, competitions and other street entertainment throughout the day in the City Centre.

SUNDAY 19 JULY

SPECTACULAR *New* EVENT FOR
WAKEFIELD CITY CENTRE **9.45**AM

✳ 'Ridings Run' - Parade of over 100 historic vehicles
from Thornes Park around the City Centre before
journeying to Elvington, near York.

✳ **City Centre** - Display of historic military vehicles
plus exhibition stands, displays and opportunities for
hands on experience with West Yorkshire Police, Fire
Service, RAF, Army, Cadets, and the Forces
Charity - SSAFA.

✳ Plus the Stewart-Ford Formula One Racing Car,
Squadronaires Marching/Display Band, Forces Bands
and other entertainment.

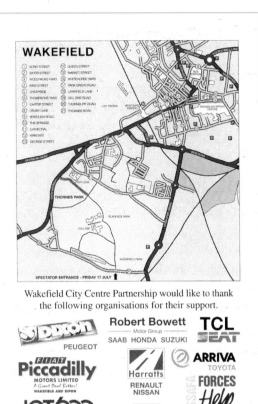

WAKEFIELD

Wakefield City Centre Partnership would like to thank
the following organisations for their support.

Programme subject to change without notice

Talk about

● What does the writer set out to do in
this leaflet?

● What features does this text have
other than just words, sentences and
paragraphs?

● What do these words mean?

**purpose   audience
persuasive language
presentational devices   lay-out
structure   headings   bullet points
fonts   frames**?

Closer reading

Word and sentence work

1 What is suggested by the use of the word 'spectacular' as a title for the event?

2 Choose three words or phrases that are particularly persuasive. Explain their effect.

3 What is 'hands on experience'? Create a word tree using 'hand' as the trunk. Add verbs, adjectives, adverbs, etc. formed from 'hand', and other examples of common uses of 'hand' combined with a preposition, e.g. 'hand in', 'hands up'.

● Make sure you understand the meaning and use of each word form you include.

4 What do you notice about the length and structure of sentences and the use of commas?

5 What contribution do headings make to the overall effect of the leaflet?

Text and genre work

6 Briefly explain what the writer is setting out to do in this leaflet and the sort of reader – the audience – it is intended for.

7 How does the choice of pictures and what they show add to the leaflet's effectiveness?

8 Why is a map and the sponsors' logos included?

9 How do the different fonts, stars and other presentational devices contribute to the leaflet's effectiveness?

10 What is your opinion of the overall structure and style of the leaflet?

● Look back at your answer to question 5. How successful is the leaflet in fulfilling its purpose?

Writing practice: leaflet design

Design a leaflet to interest people in a special event at your school, youth club or sports club. The event could be a charity week, a careers convention, or a sponsored event. The leaflet could be for pupils at your feeder schools, setting out the attractions of your school when they are old enough for transfer.

Begin by deciding:

● the main points you want to get across

● what sort of people – the audience – you want to target

- what words and phrases will have particular appeal to your audience

- what presentational devices – pictures, bullet points, headings, frames, etc. – will add to the leaflet's effectiveness

- the outline structure of your leaflet.

Follow up!

Re-design your leaflet for a totally different audience, e.g. senior citizens instead of young people, or school governors instead of parents.

Classbook reference
Unit 5, page 40

This extract forms the end of R.C. Sherriff's play *Journey's End*, which is set in the trenches during the First World War.

At this point, the fighting is increasingly serious as an offensive is launched. Stanhope, the commander of an infantry company, is in a dug-out when news comes of an injury to Raleigh. Raleigh, the son of a family friend, went to the same school as Stanhope and has always 'hero-worshipped' him.

	STANHOPE *is alone. Flying fragments of shell whistle and hiss and moan overhead. The sharp 'crack' of the rifle grenades, the thud of the shells, and the boom of the Minenwerfer mingle together in a muffled roar.* STANHOPE *takes his belt from the table and buckles it on, puts his revolver lanyard round his neck, and drops his flask and sandwiches into his pocket.*
	The SERGEANT-MAJOR *reappears and comes hurrying down the steps.*
STANHOPE	(*turning quickly*) What is it, sergeant-major?
S.-M.	Mr. Raleigh, sir –
STANHOPE	What!
S.-M.	Mr. Raleigh's been 'it, sir. Bit of shell's got 'im in the back.
STANHOPE	Badly?
S.-M.	Fraid it's broke 'is spine, sir; can't move 'is legs.
STANHOPE	Bring him down here.
S.-M.	Down 'ere, sir?
STANHOPE	(*shouting*) Yes! Down here – quickly!
	The SERGEANT-MAJOR *hurries up the steps. A shell screams and bursts very near. The* SERGEANT-MAJOR *shrinks back and throws his hand across his face, as though a human hand could ward off the hot flying pieces. He stumbles on again into the trench, and hurriedly away.*
	STANHOPE *is by* OSBORNE'S *bed, fumbling a blanket over it. He takes a trench coat off the wall and rolls it for a pillow. He goes to his own bed, takes up his blanket, and turns as the* SERGEANT-MAJOR *comes carefully down the steps carrying* RALEIGH *like a child in his huge arms.*
	(*With blanket ready.*) Lay him down there.
S.-M.	'E's fainted, sir. 'E was conscious when I picked 'im up.
	The SERGEANT-MAJOR *lays the boy gently on the bed; he draws away his hands, looks furtively at the palms, and wipes the blood on the sides of his trousers.* STANHOPE *covers* RALEIGH *with his blanket, looks intently at the boy, and turns to the* SERGEANT-MAJOR.
STANHOPE	Have they dressed the wound?

S.-M.	They've just put a pad on it, sir. Can't do no more.
Stanhope	Go at once and bring two men with a stretcher.
S.-M.	We'll never get 'im down, sir, with them shells falling on Lancers' Alley.
Stanhope	Did you hear what I said? Go and get two men with a stretcher.
S.-M.	(*after a moment's hesitation*) Very good, sir.

The Sergeant-Major goes slowly away.

Stanhope turns to Raleigh once more, then goes to the table, pushes his handkerchief into the water-jug, and brings it, wringing wet, to Raleigh's bed. He bathes the boy's face. Presently Raleigh gives a little moan, opens his eyes, and turns his head.

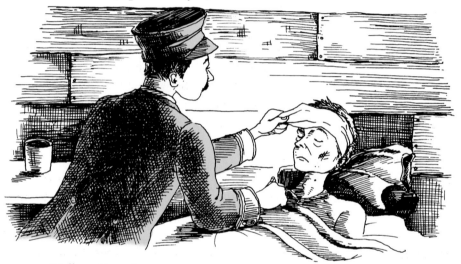

Raleigh	Hullo – Dennis –
Stanhope	Well, Jimmy – (*he smiles*) – you got one quickly. *There is silence for a while, Stanhope is sitting on a box beside Raleigh. Presently Raleigh speaks again – in a wondering voice.*
Raleigh	Why – how did I get down here?
Stanhope	Sergeant-major brought you down.

Raleigh speaks again, vaguely, trying to recollect.

Raleigh	Something – hit me in the back – knocked me clean over – sort of – winded me – I'm all right now. (*He tries to rise.*)
Stanhope	Steady, old boy. Just lie there quietly for a bit.
Raleigh	I'll be better if I get up and walk about. It happened once before – I got kicked in just the same place at Rugger; it – it soon wore off. It – it just numbs you for a bit. (*There is a pause.*) What's that rumbling noise?
Stanhope	The guns are making a bit of a row.

RALEIGH	Our guns?
STANHOPE	No. Mostly theirs.
	Again there is silence in the dug-out. A very faint rose light is beginning to glow in the dawn sky. RALEIGH *speaks again – uneasily.*
RALEIGH	I say – Dennis –
STANHOPE	Yes, old boy?
RALEIGH	It – it hasn't gone through, has it? It only just hit me? – and knocked me down?
STANHOPE	It's just gone through a bit, Jimmy.
RALEIGH	I won't have to – go on lying here?
STANHOPE	I'm going to have you taken away.
RALEIGH	Away? Where?
STANHOPE	Down to the dressing-station – then hospital – then home. (*He smiles.*) You've got a Blighty one,[1] Jimmy.
RALEIGH	But I – I can't go home just for – for a knock in the back. (*He stirs restlessly.*) I'm certain I'll be better if – if I get up. (*He tries to raise himself, and gives a sudden cry.*) Oh – God! It does hurt!
STANHOPE	It's bound to hurt, Jimmy.
RALEIGH	What's – on my legs? Something holding them down –
STANHOPE	It's all right, old chap; it's just the shock – numbed them.
	Again there is a pause. When RALEIGH *speaks, there is a different note in his voice.*
RALEIGH	It's awfully decent of you to bother, Dennis. I feel rotten lying here – everybody else – up there.
STANHOPE	It's not your fault, Jimmy.
RALEIGH	So – damn – silly – getting hit. (*Pause.*) Is there – just a drop of water?
STANHOPE	(*rising quickly*) Sure. I've got some here.
	He pours some water into the mug and brings it to RALEIGH. (*Cheerfully.*) Got some tea-leaves in it. D'you mind?
RALEIGH	No. That's all right – thanks –
	STANHOPE *holds the mug to* RALEIGH'S *lips, and the boy drinks.* I say, Dennis, don't you wait – if – if you want to be getting on.
STANHOPE	It's quite all right, Jimmy.
RALEIGH	Can you stay for a bit?
STANHOPE	Of course I can.

[1] Blighty one – Blighty meant England, and a Blighty one was a wound which would require hospital treatment in England. It was considered a piece of luck.

RALEIGH	(*faintly*) Thanks awfully.
	There is quiet in the dug-out for a long time. STANHOPE sits with one hand on RALEIGH'S arm and RALEIGH lies very still. Presently he speaks again – hardly above a whisper.
	Dennis –
STANHOPE	Yes, old boy?
RALEIGH	Could we have a light? It's – it's so frightfully dark and cold.
STANHOPE	(*rising*) Sure! I'll bring a candle and get another blanket.
	STANHOPE goes to the left-hand dug-out, and RALEIGH is alone, very still and quiet, on OSBORNE'S bed. The faint rosy glow of the dawn is deepening to an angry red. The grey night sky is dissolving, and the stars begin to go. A tiny sound comes from where RALEIGH is lying – something between a sob and a moan. STANHOPE comes back with a blanket. He takes a candle from the table and carries it to RALEIGH'S bed. He puts it on the box beside RALEIGH and speaks cheerfully.

	Is that better, Jimmy? (*RALEIGH makes no sign.*) Jimmy –
	Still RALEIGH is quiet. STANHOPE gently takes his hand. There is a long silence. STANHOPE lowers RALEIGH'S hand to the bed, rises, and takes the candle back to the table. He sits on the bench behind the table with his back to the wall, and stares listlessly across at the boy on OSBORNE'S bed. The solitary candle-flame throws up the lines on his pale, drawn face, and the dark shadows under his tired eyes. The thudding of the shells rises and falls like an angry sea.
	A PRIVATE SOLDIER comes scrambling down the steps, his round, red face wet with perspiration, his chest heaving for breath.
SOLDIER	Message from Mr. Trotter, sir – will you come at once.
	STANHOPE gazes round at the SOLDIER – and makes no other sign.
	Mr. Trotter, sir – says will you come at once!
	STANHOPE rises stiffly and takes his helmet from the table.

| STANHOPE | All right, Broughton, I'm coming. |

The SOLDIER turns and goes away.

STANHOPE pauses for a moment by OSBORNE'S bed and lightly runs his fingers over RALEIGH'S tousled hair. He goes stiffly up the steps, his tall figure black against the dawn sky.

The shelling has risen to a great fury. The solitary candle burns with a steady flame, and RALEIGH lies in the shadows. The whine of a shell rises to a shriek and bursts on the dug-out roof. The shock stabs out the candle-flame; the timber props of the door cave slowly in, sandbags fall and block the passage to the open air.

There is darkness in the dug-out. Here and there the red dawn glows through the jagged holes of the broken doorway.

Very faintly there comes the dull rattle of machine-guns and the fevered spatter of rifle fire.

THE PLAY ENDS

Talk about

- How far is it true that stage directions are written as much to create a picture of the scene in a reader's mind as to provide instructions for the set designers of a production?

- How may 'normal' conversations, usually consisting of short or broken sentences, be written into a play without losing its sense or becoming boring?

- What do these words mean?
dialogue cliché understatement Army slang standard English accent mood dramatic effect climax

- Identify examples of the use of **clichés** and **understatement** in this extract. Discuss the significance of these words in their context, and think about how they might be spoken on stage to convey that significance.

- Identify and discuss examples of moments when what is left unsaid, or is hidden behind familiar phrases, is also significant.

Closer reading

Word and sentence work

1 Dashes are frequently used between words and phrases in Raleigh's speeches.

- What effect do they convey?

2 Stanhope tells Raleigh to 'lie there quietly for **a bit**'; that the 'guns are making **a bit** of a row'; that the shell wound has 'gone through **a bit**'.

- What effect is his use of '**a bit**' intended to have in these contexts?

3 How do the first set of stage directions give an impression of the noise and confusion of battle?

4 How does the writer suggest that the Sergeant Major (SM) speaks in a different accent from Stanhope?

5 From what the Sergeant Major says, how badly do you think Raleigh is wounded?

Text and genre work

6 What do Stanhope's actions, before Raleigh regains consciousness, suggest about his attitude towards him?

7 What impression is Raleigh trying to give when he compares the wound to a 'kick in just the same place at Rugger'?

8 What evidence is there that the wound is a very serious and painful one?

9 What is the significance of Raleigh asking for a light and the flickering candle beside his bed?

10 How effective is this scene as the ending to the play? Think about the effects created by:
- what the characters say and do
- the stage directions and how they describe the setting and the sound effects
- the use of 'props' – bits of equipment, furniture etc.

Writing practice: waiting

Create a short play scene from a very simple situation, e.g. you are waiting for a tense interview with someone in authority – a senior teacher, sports club leader, or parent.

- Think about how you would use stage directions to set the scene. It can be somewhere quite familiar, but perhaps, on this occasion, you are more aware than usual of certain aspects of your surroundings.

- Think about your actions. How might they express your inner fears/tension/hopes? You could speak some of your thoughts aloud, or practise what you will say when you finally go into the interview.

- Perhaps other people walk by as you wait, stopping for a word – of encouragement? or sympathy? or mockery?

- Perhaps you notice objects, things or people that seem significant, even ominous, in your present situation.

- Try to build up to a climax at the end. You could use a simple idea such as 'The door opened', or ' "Come in," called a voice.'

Follow up!

Read the play script you have written again. Now write a short piece of dialogue between yourself and a friend, **after the event**, explaining what actually happened and how you suffered.

Classbook reference
Unit 11, page 106

Here are two pieces of writing about chimpanzees. The first extract is from a book, *A Zoo in my Luggage,* in which Gerald Durrell describes encounters with various species from the natural world in many different places – in this passage, the story of Cholmondeley, ´Chumley´. The second passage is taken from a website about chimpanzees and describes how they use tools and communicate.

Extract A

The Life and Death of Cholmondeley

Shortly before we left our hill-top hut at Bakebe and travelled down to our last camp at Kumba, we had to stay with us a most unusual guest in the shape of Cholmondeley, known to his friends as Chumley.

Chumley was a full-grown chimpanzee; his owner, a District Officer, was finding the ape's large size rather awkward, and he wanted to send him to London Zoo as a present, so that he could visit the animal when he was back in England on leave. He wrote asking us if we would mind taking Chumley back with us when we left, and depositing him at his new home in London, and we replied that we would not mind at all. I don't think that either John or myself had the least idea how big Chumley was: I know that I visualised an ape of about three years old, standing about three feet high. I got a rude shock when Chumley moved in.

He arrived in the back of a small van, seated sedately in a huge crate. When the doors of his crate where opened and Chumley stepped out with all the ease and self-confidence of a film star, I was considerably shaken for, standing on his bow legs in a normal slouching chimp position, he came up to my waist, and if he had straightened up, his head would have been on a level with my chest. He had huge arms, and must have measured at least twice my measurements round his hairy chest. Owing to bad tooth growth both sides of his face were swollen out of all proportion, and this gave him a weird pugilistic look. His eyes were small, deep set, and intelligent; the top of his head was nearly bald owing, I discovered later, to his habit of sitting and rubbing the palms of his hand backwards across his head, an exercise which seemed to afford him much pleasure and which he persisted in until the top of his skull was quite devoid of hair. This was no young chimp as I had expected, but a veteran of about eight or nine years old, fully mature, strong as a powerful man and, to judge by his expression, with considerable experience of life. Although he was not exactly a nice chimp to look at (I had seen more handsome), he certainly had a terrific personality: it hit you as soon as you set eyes on him. His little eyes looked at you with a great intelligence, and there seemed to be a glitter of ironic laughter in their depths that made one feel uncomfortable.

He stood on the ground and

surveyed his surroundings with a shrewd glance, and then he turned to me and held out one of his soft, pink-palmed hands to be shaken, with exactly that bored expression that one sees on the faces of professional hand-shakers. Round his neck was a thick chain, and its length drooped over the tailboard of the lorry and disappeared into the depths of his crate. With an animal of less personality than Chumley, this would have been a sign of his subjugation, of his captivity. But Chumley wore the chain with the superb air of a Lord Mayor; after shaking my hand so professionally, he turned and proceeded to pull the chain, which measured some fifteen feet, out of his crate. He gathered it up carefully into loops, hung it over one hand and proceeded to walk into the hut as if he owned it. Thus, in the first few minutes of arrival, Chumley had made us feel inferior, and had moved in not, we felt, because we wanted it, but because he did. I almost felt I ought to apologise for the mess on the table when he walked in.

He seated himself in a chair, dropped his chain on the floor, and then looked hopefully at me. It was quite obvious that he expected some sort of refreshment after his tiring journey. I roared out to the kitchen for them to make a cup of tea, for I had been warned that Chumley had a great liking for the cup that cheers. Leaving him sitting in the chair and surveying our humble abode with ill-concealed disgust, I went out to his crate, and in it I found a tin plate and a battered tin mug of colossal proportions. When I returned to the hut bearing these Chumley brightened considerably, and even went so far as to praise me for my intelligence.

'Ooooooo, umph!' he said, and then crossed his legs and continued his inspection of the hut. I sat down opposite him and produced a packet of cigarettes. As I was selecting one, a long black arm was stretched across the table, and Chumley grunted in delight. Wondering what he would do I handed him a cigarette, and to my astonishment he put it carefully in the corner of his mouth. I lit my smoke and handed Chumley the matches, thinking that this would fool him. He opened the box, took out a match, struck it, lit his cigarette, threw the matches down on the table, crossed his legs again, and lay back in his chair inhaling thankfully, and blowing clouds of smoke out of his nose. Obviously he had vices in his make-up of which I had been kept in ignorance.

Just at that moment Pious entered, bearing the tray of tea: the effect on him when he saw me sitting at the table with the chimp, smoking and apparently exchanging gossip, was considerable.

'Eh …eahh!' he gasped, backing away.

'Whar … hooo,' said Chumley, sighting the tea and waving one hand madly.

'Na whatee that, sah?' asked Pious, from the doorway.

'This is Chumley,' I explained, 'he won't hurt you. Put the tea on the table.'

Pious did as he was told and then retreated to the door again. As I poured tea and milk into Chumley's mug, and added three tablespoons of sugar, he watched me with a glittering eye, and made a soft 'ooing' noise to himself. I handed him the mug and he took it carefully in both hands. There was a

moment's confusion when he tried to rid himself of the cigarette, which he found he could not hold as well as the mug; he solved the problem by placing the cigarette on the table. Then he tested the tea carefully with one lip stuck out, to see if it was too hot. As it was, he sat there and blew on it until it was the right temperature, and then he drank it down. When he had finished the liquid there still remained the residue of syrupy sugar at the bottom, and as Chumley's motto was obviously waste not want not, he balanced the mug on his nose and kept it there until the last of the sugar had trickled down into his mouth. Then he held it out for a refill.

Chumley was, I think, a little jealous of Sue,[1] but he was too much of a gentleman to show it. Not long after her arrival, however, London's Zoo's official collector arrived in the Cameroons, and with great regret I handed Chumley over to be transported back to England. I did not see him again for over four months, and then I went to visit him in the sanatorium at Regent's Park. He had

a great straw-filled room to live in, and was immensely popular with the sanatorium staff. I did not think that he would recognise me, for when he had last seen me I had been clad in tropical kit and sporting a beard and moustache, and now I was clean-shaven and wearing a garb of a civilised man. But recognise me he did, for he whirled around his room like a dervish when he saw me and then came rushing across to give me his old greeting, gently biting my finger. We sat in the straw and I gave him some sugar I had brought for him, and then we smoked a cigarette together while he removed my shoes and socks and examined my feet and legs to make sure there was nothing wrong with them. Then he took his cigarette butt and carefully put it out in the corner of his room, well away from his straw. When the time came to go, he shook hands with me formally and watched my departure through the crack in the door. Shortly after he was moved to the monkey-house, and so he could receive no more visitors in his private room.

I never saw Chumley again, but I know his history: he became a great television star, going down to Alexandra Palace and doing his act in front of the cameras like an old trouper. Then his teeth started to worry him, and so he was moved from the monkey-house back to the sanatorium to have an operation. One day, feeling bored with life, he broke out and sallied forth across Regent's Park. When he reached the main road he found a bus conveniently at hand, so he swung himself aboard; but his presence caused

[1] A very young chimp, who later came to stay.

such horror amongst the occupants of the bus that he got excited and forgot himself so far as to bite someone.

If only people would realize that to scream and panic is the best way of provoking an attack from any wild animal. Leaving the bus and its now bloodstained passengers, Chumley walked down the road, made a pass at a lady with a pram (who nearly fainted) and was wandering about to see what else he could do to liven life up for Londoners, when a member of the sanatorium's staff arrived on the scene. By now I expect Chumley had realised that civilised people were no decent company for a well-brought-up chimp, so he took his keeper's hand and walked back home. After this he was branded as not safe and sent back to the monkey-house. But he had not finished with publicity yet, for some time later he had to go back to the sanatorium for yet more treatment on his teeth, and he decided to repeat his little escapade.

It was Christmas Eve and Chumley obviously had memories of other and more convivial festivities, probably spent at some club in the depths of Africa. Anyway, he decided that if he had a walk round London on Christmas Eve, season of goodwill, he might run across someone who would offer him a beer. So he broke open his cage and set off once more across Regent's Park. At Gloucester Gate he looked about hopefully for a bus, but there was not one in sight. But there were some cars parked there and Chumley approached them and beat on the doors vigorously, in the hope that the occupants would open up and offer him a lift. Chumley loved a ride in any sort of conveyance. But the foolish humans misconstrued his actions: there he was full of Christmas spirit, asking for a lift, and all they could do was to wind up their windows and yell for help. This, thought Chumley, was a damn poor way to show a fellow the traditional British hospitality. But before he had time to explain his mission to the car owners, a panting posse of keepers arrived, and he was bundled back to the Zoo. Chumley had escaped twice, and they were not going to risk it happening again: from being a fine, intelligent animal, good enough to be displayed on television, he had suddenly become (by reason of his escapades) a fierce and untrustworthy monster; he might escape yet again and bite some worthy citizen, so rather than risk this, Chumley was sentenced to death and shot.

Gerald Durrell

Extract B

Chimpanzees' Tool Use, Culture and Communication

For many years, humans had distinguished themselves from the rest of the animal world by their ability to make and use tools. In the 1960s, this distinction was shattered when Dr Jane Goodall reported several observations of chimpanzees making and using tools. She learned that chimpanzees not only used various tools for different tasks, but modified objects for tools so that they were better suited for the tasks. Humans were faced with the fact that they were not as far from their primate relatives as they had liked to believe.

In the forests of Tanzania, Dr Goodall observed chimpanzees carefully choosing sticks and then stripping them of their leaves so that they could be used to fish for termites and ants. The twigs are broken, shaped with fingers and teeth, and inserted into termite mounds to capture insects whose bites are very painful. The termites attack and cling to the stick, allowing the chimpanzee to quickly pull the stick out and eat the termites. The use of a twig as a tool allows the chimpanzee to avoid being stung.

Almost as fascinating as the fact that they make and use these sticks for tools is the process by which they learn to do so. Chimpanzees are not born with these skills; they must learn them by watching adults, usually their mothers. Female chimpanzees seem to have more success in termite fishing, perhaps only because they are more patient during the learning process and do not give up frustrated, as the males are apt to do.

Termite fishing is not the only example of tool use in chimpanzees. In addition, leaves are chewed until softened and used for sponges to clean wounds or to absorb liquids for ingesting. Certain groups of chimpanzees use rocks as hammers and anvils to crack open palm nuts so they can eat the meat inside. One troop of chimpanzees has been observed using pieces of bark to protect their hands and feet as they climb trees with prickly branches. Chimpanzees sometimes eat plants that they would normally avoid because they are hard to swallow or bitter. Research has shown that these plants have medicinal qualities, such as controlling intestinal parasites.

The differences in tool use between different troops of chimpanzees can be seen as a form of culture. There are many groups of chimpanzees who have access to palm nuts and rocks and yet do not engage in nut cracking. The techniques used for termite fishing differs between groups of chimpanzees. Some will use a short stick which they use to collect the termites and then remove the termites with their mouths. Others choose a longer stick and quickly sweep the termites off the twig with their hands and then into their mouths. Just as in humans, much of the chimpanzee behaviour is learned and passed down from generation to generation.

Because chimpanzees are extremely intelligent, scientists wondered if they could produce human language. We know that communication between non-human primates is restricted to information that can be conveyed using a small number of sounds. These sounds are used for specific events or behaviours. For example, when a chimpanzee finds a tree with ripe fruit, it gets excited and makes grunting sounds or food grunts. This type of sound is always associated with food and excitement because non-human primate communication originates in the limbic system, an area of the brain that regulates hormones, heart and respiration activity. Damage to this area of the brain will result in deficits in the production of facial expressions, such as fear grins, which are linked to emotional states.

Chimpanzees make loud piercing calls called 'pant-hoots', which carry long distances to identify the individual. If a chimpanzee hears a stranger pant-hoot, it may wait silently and alertly to learn if more strangers are nearby before proceeding on its way. Pant-hoots may be voiced in a variety of emotional situations: inquiring as to the identity of another chimpanzee, finding a food source or when feeding, during the social excitement of reunions, or in times of fear.

Communication studies, using non-human primates as subjects, focused on symbolic language due to the differences in human and chimpanzee anatomy. Some laboratory chimpanzees and gorillas have been taught ASL (American Sign Language of the Deaf) and symbolic computer languages. These apes learned to make and to read several hundred signs correctly. In addition, they spontaneously invented new signs to communicate information, voiced wants, needs and emotions. The results of these studies suggest that structures in the human brain capable of producing language also exist in the brain of non-human primates in a rudimentary form.

Talk about

- What is your attitude towards animals and keeping them as pets or in zoos?

- What is each writer's attitude towards and relationship with the chimpanzees?

- What do these words mean?
  active/passive voice
  personal response
  objective/formal tone
  adjectives and adverbs
  tone
  genre
  simple/complex sentences

Closer reading

Word and sentence work

1 List six adjectives from Extract A that are used to describe Chumley, e.g. 'pugilistic', 'veteran'.

- Explain what each word means and the impression it creates.

2 Select three phrases or sentences from Extract A that make Chumley sound more like a man than an animal.

- How do these phrases or sentences help to make the picture of Chumley clearer and more interesting?

3 What differences do you notice about the verb forms in Extract B compared with Extract A?

- Give some examples and try to explain their effect.

4 What is the difference between the language used in Extract B to describe the behaviour of the chimpanzees, and the language in Extract A?

- Look particularly at the choice of adjectives, verbs and adverbs.

5 In the final part of Extract A, Chumley's break-outs are called 'little escapades'.

- What does this suggest the author felt about them?

- How do you think the people involved might have felt?

Text and genre work

6 If you were drawing a cartoon of Chumley, how would you portray him?

- What features would you emphasise and exaggerate for comic effect?

7 What impression do you get of the character of the narrator in Extract A and his attitude towards Chumley?

- What does he say and do that gives you this impression?

8 Look carefully at Extract B. Three of the paragraphs about tool use and culture begin:
  'Almost as fascinating as the fact...'
  'Termite fishing is not the only example...'
  'The differences in tool use...'

- How do these sentences help to structure the text and make it easier to understand?

9 The writers of these two extracts have very different purposes in mind.

- What do you think they each set out to do in their writing?

10 These two extracts are from texts of a different type or **genre**.

- Explain as accurately as you can what you think are the obvious features of tone and style that are typical of each genre.

Writing practice: an encounter with an animal

Most people have a pet at some stage in their lives or encounter other people's animals.

Write two short pieces about an animal or creature you know well.

- In the first piece, try to describe the animal as objectively as you can. Give details of its characteristics, lifestyle, habitat, ways of communicating, etc.

- In the second piece, try to bring out something of the animal's character. You could make it sound much more 'human' by describing one or two interesting or amusing incidents which reflect its 'personality'.

- Try to make your two pieces of writing very different from each other in style and tone.

- This frame may help you to plan your writing:

Ideas	Objective account	Personal account
Animal (e.g. hedgehog)	Type/genus (e.g. mammal)	Name (e.g. Hogwash)
Habitat	e.g. hedgerows	e.g. our back garden
Lifestyle	e.g. scavenging	e.g. likes to eat our cat's tea from its saucer
Way of communicating, etc.		

Follow up!

Read the first chapter of *Hard Times* by Charles Dickens. What do you learn about the difference between knowing **about** something and knowing the **definition** of something?

Classbook reference
Unit 7, page 57

Read this poem by Thomas Hood, who lived from 1799–1845.

Faithless Nellie Gray

Ben Battle was a soldier bold,
    And used to war's alarms;
But a cannon-ball took off his legs,
    So he laid down his arms.

Now as they bore him off the field,
    Said he, 'Let others shoot,
For here I leave my second leg,
    And the Forty-second Foot!'

The army-surgeons made him limbs:
    Said he: – 'They're only pegs:
But there's as wooden members quite
    As represent my legs!'

Now Ben he loved a pretty maid,
    Her name was Nellie Gray:
So he went to pay her his devours
    When he'd devoured his pay!

But when he called on Nellie Gray,
    She made him quite a scoff;
And when she saw his wooden legs
    Began to take them off!

'O, Nellie Gray! O, Nellie Gray!
    Is this your love so warm?
The love that loves a scarlet coat
    Should be more uniform!'

She said, 'I loved a soldier once,
    For he was blythe and brave;
But I will never have a man
    With both legs in the grave!

'Before you had those timber toes,
    Your love I did allow,
But then, you know, you stand upon
    Another footing now!'

'O, Nellie Gray! O, Nellie Gray!
    For all your jeering speeches,
At duty's call, I left my legs
    In Badajos's *breaches*!'

'Why, then,' she said, 'you've lost the feet
    Of legs in war's alarms,
And now you cannot wear your shoes
    Upon your feats of arms!'

'Oh, false and fickle Nellie Gray;
    I know why you refuse:
Though I've no feet – some other man
    Is standing in my shoes!

'I wish I ne'er had seen your face;
    But now, a long farewell!
For you will be my death, alas!
    You will not be my *Nell*!'

Now when he went from Nellie Gray,
    His heart so heavy got –
And life was such a burthen grown,
    It made him take a knot!

So round his melancholy neck,
    A rope he did entwine,
And, for his second time in life,
    Enlisted in the Line!

One end he tied around a beam,
    And then removed his pegs,
And as his legs were off, – of course,
    He soon was off his legs!

And there he hung, till he was dead
    As any nail in town, –
For though distress had cut him up,
    It could not cut him down!

A dozen men sat on his corpse,
    To find out why he died –
And they buried Ben in four cross-roads,
    With a *stake* in his inside!

Thomas Hood

Talk about

- What is meant by **rhyme** and **rhythm**? Discuss examples from poems you have previously read.

- What are **puns**, '**double entendres**' and **plays on words**? Discuss some examples.

  - What do these words mean?
  literary device
  alliteration
  simile
  metaphor
  verse/stanza
  personification
  literal/metaphorical/figurative meaning

Closer reading

1 What does the title suggest about the subject matter and tone of the poem?

2 What does the name 'Ben Battle' suggest about the main character?

- What effect does it have on you and your expectations?

3 How far does the first verse confirm the impression you gained from the title?

- What confirms or changes your impression – words, verse-form, rhymes?

4 In verse 4, the word 'devours' is used in a now out-dated sense to mean 'devotions'.

- Explain the play on words in the last two lines of this verse.

5 How is humour created by the words 'you stand upon another footing...' (verse 8) and '...standing in my shoes' (verse 11)?

6 Explain the ambiguity – and humour – in the use of the word 'breaches' (verse 9).

7 What does 'enlisted in the line' (verse 14) usually mean?

- What does it mean in this poem?

8 How does the use of the words 'cut up' (last verse but one) contribute to the humour of the final verse?

9 Why do you think Hood ends so many lines and verses with exclamation marks?

- What is their effect?

10 Think about the rhythm and rhyming pattern of the poem. What do they contribute to its overall effect?

Writing practice: wit and word play

Write some verses of your own, imitating the rhyming pattern and rhythm of Hood's poem.

- You might find it helpful to begin by writing down:
  – phrases that are used **figuratively** as well as **literally**, e.g. come round, take a trip, pass away/on
  – words that sound alike but have different meanings, e.g. wait/weight, see/sea, fate/fete.

- There can be confusion between names, e.g:
    - 'born in March' could refer to the month or the town
    - George Cross could be a person or a medal.

- You could use these to create **plays on words**. For example:

'There's an elephant stuck in a tree over there!'
Said Bill, a bit of a clown.
'But scratch my head and think as I may,
I can't work out how we might get it down.'

'You are a fool,' said his good friend Ben,
'And you really talk some junk!
Go across to it now, take a very firm grip,
And shake it hard by the trunk!'

- If you write three or four separate verses, you might find a way to link them together into a longer 'story'.

Follow up!

Look at another of Hood's comic poems, for example *Sally Brown* or *The Poacher*.

- Pick out all the words and phrases that are ambiguous.

- How are these used for comic effect?

- Make up some similar verses or riddles involving word play. For example:

    a) Old Mr Wong from far Hong Kong
        Had teeth old, worn and dirty.
        The dentist asked, 'Can you come today?'
        Mr Wong said, 'Yes, tooth hurtie.' *   (*2.30!)

    b) Fred Flintlock was a teacher bold,
        His fierceness famed in fable;
        He taught the kids about Adam's sons,
        And caned when he was able! *   (* See Genesis, Chapter 4)

Classbook reference
Unit 15,
page 158

Both these passages focus on a view over the River Thames and London in the nineteenth century. The first is a sonnet written by Wordsworth at the turn of the eighteenth century; the second is an extract from *The Morning Chronicle* written by Henry Mayhew about 50 years later. Wordsworth's viewpoint is Westminster Bridge; Mayhew's is a little further downstream, at St Paul's.

Composed upon Westminster Bridge

Earth has not anything to show more fair:
Dull would he be of soul who could pass by
A sight so touching in its majesty:
This City now doth like a garment wear
The beauty of the morning; silent, bare,
Ships, towers, domes, theatres, and temples lie
Open unto the fields, and to the sky;
All bright and glittering in the smokeless air.
Never did sun more beautifully steep
In his first splendour, valley, rock, or hill;
Ne'er saw I, never felt, a calm so deep!
The river glideth at his own sweet will:
Dear God! the very houses seem asleep;
And all that mighty heart is lying still.

William Wordsworth

The Thames from St Paul's

In the hope of obtaining a bird's-eye view of the port, I went up to the Golden Gallery that is immediately below the ball of St Paul's. It was noon, and an exquisitely bright and clear spring day; but the view was smudgy and smeared with smoke. And yet the haze which hung like a curtain of shadow before and over everything, increased rather than diminished the giant sublimity of the city that lay stretched out beneath. It was utterly unlike London as seen every day below, in all its bricken and hard-featured reality; it was rather the phantasm – the spectral illusion, as it were, of the

great metropolis – such as one might see in a dream, with here and there stately churches and palatial hospitals, shimmering like white marble, their windows glittering in the sunshine like plates of burnished gold – while the rest of the scene was all hazy and indefinite. Even the outlines of the neighbouring streets, steeples, and towers were blurred in misty indistinctness. Clumps of buildings and snatches of parks looked through the clouds like dim islands rising out of the sea of smoke. It was impossible to tell where the sky ended and the city began; and as you peered into the thick haze you could, after a time, make out the dusky figures of tall factory chimneys plumed with black smoke; while spires and turrets seemed to hang midway between you and the earth, as if poised in the thick grey air. In the distance the faint hills, with the sun shining upon them, appeared like some far-off shore, or a mirage seen in the sky – indeed, the whole scene was more like the view of some imaginary and romantic Cloudland, than that of the most matter-of-fact and prosaic city in the world. As you peeped down into the thoroughfares you could see streams of busy little men, like ants, continually hurrying along in opposite directions; while, what with carts, cabs, and omnibuses, the earth seemed all alive with tiny creeping things, as when one looks into the grass on a summer's day. As you listened you caught the roar of the restless human tide of enterprise and competition at work below; and as you turned to contemplate the river at your back, you saw the sunlight shining upon the grey water beneath you like a sheet of golden tissue, while far away in the distance it sparkled again as the stream went twisting through the monster town. Beyond London-bridge nothing was visible; a thick veil of haze and fog hung before the shipping, so that not one solitary mast was to be seen marking the far-famed port of London. And yet one would hardly have had it otherwise! To behold the metropolis without its smoke – with its thousand steeples standing out against the clear blue sky sharp and definite in their outlines – is to see London as it is not – without its native element. But as the vast city lay there beneath me, half hid in mist and with only glimpses of its greatness visible, it had a much more sublime and ideal effect from the very inability to grasp the whole of its literal reality.

Talk about

- What features of the scene do both descriptions have in common?

- What other details does each writer pick out to describe?

- How do the different **genres** create different impressions of the scene?

- What do these words mean?
  traditional verse forms
  characteristics
  critical
  selective
  use of detail

Closer reading

Look at Wordsworth's poem:

1 The poem is in the form of a **sonnet**.

- What do you know about sonnets?

- What does this suggest about Wordsworth's attitude to his subject?

2 What do the **images** 'doth like a garment wear' and a 'mighty heart' suggest about the way the poet thinks of 'this City'?

3 What effects are achieved by the repetition of the word 'Never' and by placing it at the beginning of a line?

4 What impression is created by the use of **abstract nouns**?

- How is this supported by Wordsworth's choice of **adjectives** and **adverbs**?

Look at Mayhew's description:

5 Find examples and compare Mayhew's choice of **abstract nouns**, **adjectives** and **adverbs** with Wordsworth's.

6 Look back to your answer to question 2.

- Explain any similarities or differences between the way Wordsworth and Mayhew think of the city.

7 What aspects of city life does Mayhew describe that Wordsworth ignores?

- What do these contribute to his picture of the city?

8 Look at the length and structure of the **sentences** in this passage.

- How do they reflect the picture that Mayhew is creating?

Consider both texts:

9 What differences in tense and endings do you notice in the verb forms in these two pieces?

- Can you say the two writers have different purposes?

- What are they?

10 What strengths, as a piece of writing, does Wordsworth's sonnet have – with its rhyming pattern and other poetic devices – that Mayhew's longer description lacks?

● Does Mayhew create a more – or less – effective picture of London than Wordsworth? How?

Writing practice: the place where I live

Write a description of a place you know well. It may be your city, town or village (or a part of them), or simply a 'scene'. Bring out its unusual beauty, mystery or special quality at the moment you capture it.

● Think about the details you might include. How will these look? What effect will they have, depending on how you combine them in your writing?

● Choose words and sentence structures carefully so you create a real sense of what you see in your mind's eye.

Follow up!

What would you see if you were 'facing the other way' or looking at the same scene at a different time of the day or year? Write a second description that contrasts with the first.

Classbook reference
Unit 10, page 93

This passage is an extract from the opening chapters of *Vanity Fair* by William Thackeray. It is set in the early years of the nineteenth century and describes the final departure of Amelia Sedley and Becky Sharp, two young girls, from their school, Miss Pinkerton's academy for young ladies.

Vanity Fair
A NOVEL WITHOUT A HERO
CHAPTER 1
CHISWICK MALL

WHILE the present century was in its teens, and on one sunshiny morning in June, there drove up to the great iron gate of Miss Pinkerton's academy for young ladies, on Chiswick Mall, a large family coach, with two fat horses in blazing harness, driven by a fat coachman in a three-cornered hat and wig, at the rate of four miles an hour. A black servant, who reposed on the box beside the fat coachman, uncurled his bandy legs as soon as the equipage drew up opposite Miss Pinkerton's shining brass plate, and as he pulled the bell, at least a score of young heads were seen peering out of the narrow windows of the stately old brick house. Nay, the acute observer might have recognised the little red nose of good-natured Miss Jemima Pinkerton herself, rising over some geranium-pots in the window of that lady's own drawing-room.

'It is Mrs. Sedley's coach, sister,' said Miss Jemima. 'Sambo, the black servant, has just rung the bell; and the coachman has a new red waistcoat.'

'Have you completed all the necessary preparations incident to Miss Sedley's departure, Miss Jemima?' asked Miss Pinkerton herself, that majestic lady; the Semiramis of Hammersmith, the friend of Doctor Johnson, the correspondent of Mrs. Chapone herself.

'The girls were up at four this morning, packing her trunks, sister,' replied Miss Jemima; 'we have made her a bow-pot.'

'Say a bouquet, sister Jemima, 'tis more genteel.'

Miss Pinkerton proceeded to write her own name, and Miss Sedley's, in the fly-leaf of a Johnson's Dictionary – the interesting work which she invariably presented to her scholars on their departure from the Mall. On the cover was inserted a copy of 'Lines addressed to a young lady on quitting Miss Pinkerton's school, at the Mall; by the late revered Doctor Samuel Johnson.' In fact, the Lexicographer's name was always on the lips of this majestic woman, and a visit he had paid to her was the cause of her reputation and her fortune.

Being commanded by her elder sister to get 'the Dictionary' from the cupboard, Miss Jemima had extracted two copies of the book from the receptacle in question. When Miss Pinkerton had finished the inscription in the first, Jemima, with rather a dubious and timid air, handed her the second.

'For whom is this, Miss Jemima?' said Miss Pinkerton, with awful coldness.

'For Becky Sharp,' answered Jemima, trembling very much, and blushing over her withered face and neck, as she turned her back on her sister. 'For Becky Sharp: she's going too.'

'MISS JEMIMA!' exclaimed Miss Pinkerton, in the largest capitals. 'Are you in your senses? Replace the Dictionary in the closet, and never venture to take such a liberty in future.'

'Well, sister, it's only two-and-ninepence, and poor Becky will be miserable if she don't get one.'

'Send Miss Sedley instantly to me,' said Miss Pinkerton. And so, venturing not to say another word, poor Jemima trotted off, exceedingly flurried and nervous.

Well, then. The flowers, and the presents, and the trunks, and bonnet-boxes of Miss Sedley having been arranged by Mr. Sambo in the carriage, together with a very small and weather-beaten old cow's-skin trunk with Miss Sharp's card neatly nailed upon it, which was delivered by Sambo with a grin, and packed by the coachman with a corresponding sneer – the hour for parting came; and the grief of that moment was considerably lessened by the admirable discourse which Miss Pinkerton addressed to her pupil. Not that the parting speech caused Amelia to philosophise, or that it armed her in any way with a calmness, the result of argument; but it was intolerably dull, pompous, and tedious; and having the fear of her schoolmistress greatly before her eyes, Miss Sedley did not venture, in her presence, to give way to any ebullitions of private grief. A seed-cake and a bottle of wine were produced in the drawing-room, as on the solemn occasions of the visits of parents, and these refreshments being partaken of, Miss Sedley was at liberty to depart.

'You'll go in and say good-bye to Miss Pinkerton, Becky!' said Miss Jemima to a young lady of whom nobody took any notice, and who was coming downstairs with her own bandbox.

'I suppose I must,' said Miss Sharp calmly, and much to the

wonder of Miss Jemima; and the latter having knocked at the door, and receiving permission to come in, Miss Sharp advanced in a very unconcerned manner, and said in French, and with a perfect accent, '*Mademoiselle, je viens vous faire mes adieux.*'

Miss Pinkerton did not understand French; she only directed those who did; but biting her lips and throwing up her venerable and Roman-nosed head (on the top of which figured a large solemn turban), she said, 'Miss Sharp, I wish you a good-morning.' As the Hammersmith Semiramis spoke she waved one hand, both by way of adieu, and to give Miss Sharp an opportunity of shaking one of the fingers of the hand which was left out for that purpose.

Miss Sharp only folded her own hands with a very frigid smile and bow, and quite declined to accept the proffered honour; on which Semiramis tossed up her turban more indignantly than ever. In fact, it was a little battle between the young lady and the old one, and the latter was worsted. 'Heaven bless you, my child,' said she, embracing Amelia, and scowling the while over the girl's shoulder at Miss Sharp. 'Come away, Becky,' said Miss Jemima, pulling the young woman away in great alarm, and the drawing-room door closed upon them for ever.

Then came the struggle and parting below. Words refuse to tell it. All the servants were there in the hall – all the dear friends – all the young ladies – the dancing-master who had just arrived; and there was such a scuffling, and hugging, and kissing, and crying, with the hysterical *yoops* of Miss Swartz, the parlour-boarder, from her room, as no pen can depict, and as the tender heart would fain pass over. The embracing was over; they parted – that is, Miss Sedley parted from her friends. Miss Sharp had demurely entered the carriage some minutes before. Nobody cried for leaving *her*.

Sambo of the bandy-legs slammed the carriage-door on his young weeping mistress. He sprang up behind the carriage. 'Stop!' cried Miss Jemima, rushing to the gate with a parcel.

'It's some sandwiches, my dear,' said she to Amelia. 'You may be hungry, you know; and Becky, Becky Sharp, here's a book for you that my sister – that is, I – Johnson's Dictionary, you know; you mustn't leave us without that. Good-bye. Drive on, coachman. God bless you!'

And the kind creature retreated into the garden, overcome with emotion.

But, lo! and just as the coach drove off, Miss Sharp put her pale face out of the window and actually flung the book back into the garden.

This almost caused Jemima to faint with terror. 'Well, I never,' – said she – ' what an audacious' – Emotion prevented her from completing either sentence. The carriage rolled away; the great gates were closed; the bell rang for the dancing lesson. The world is before the two young ladies; and so, farewell to Chiswick Mall.

CHAPTER 2

IN WHICH MISS SHARP AND MISS SEDLEY PREPARE TO OPEN THE CAMPAIGN

WHEN Miss Sharp had performed the heroical act mentioned in the last chapter, and had seen the Dictionary, flying over the pavement of the little garden, fall at length at the feet of the astonished Miss Jemima, the young lady's countenance, which had before worn an almost livid look of hatred, assumed a smile that perhaps was scarcely more agreeable, and she sank back in the carriage in an easy frame of mind, saying, 'So much for the Dictionary; and, thank God, I'm out of Chiswick.'

Miss Sedley was almost as flurried at the act of defiance as Miss Jemima had been; for, consider, it was but one minute that she had left school, and the impressions of six years are not got over in that space of time. Nay, with some persons those awes and terrors of youth last for ever and ever. I know, for instance, an old gentleman of sixty-eight, who said to me one morning at breakfast, with a very agitated countenance, 'I dreamed last night that I was flogged by Dr. Raine.' Fancy had carried him back five-and-fifty years in the course of that evening. Dr. Raine and his rod were just as awful to him in his heart, then, at sixty-eight, as they had been at thirteen. If the Doctor, with a large birch, had appeared bodily to him, even at the age of threescore and eight, and had said in awful voice, 'Boy, take down your pant ***?' Well, well, Miss Sedley was exceedingly alarmed at this act of insubordination.

'How could you do so, Rebecca?' at last she said, after a pause.

'Why, do you think Miss Pinkerton will come out and order me back to the black hole?' said Rebecca, laughing.

'No: but' –

'I hate the whole house,' continued Miss Sharp in a fury. 'I hope I may never set eyes on it again. I wish it were in the bottom of the Thames, I do; and if Miss Pinkerton were there, I wouldn't pick her out, that I wouldn't. O how I should like to see her floating in the water yonder, turban and all, with her train streaming after her, and her nose like the beak of a wherry!'

'Hush!' cried Miss Sedley.

'Why, will the black footman tell tales?' cried Miss Rebecca, laughing. 'He may go back and tell Miss Pinkerton that I hate her with all my soul, and I wish he would; and I wish I had a means of proving it, too. For two years I have only had insults and outrage from her. I have been treated worse than any servant in the kitchen. I have never had a friend or a kind word, except from you. I have been made to tend the little girls in the lower schoolroom, and to talk French to the Misses, until I grew sick of my mother-tongue. But that talking French to Miss Pinkerton was capital fun, wasn't it? She doesn't know a word of French, and was too proud to confess it. I believe it was that which made her part with me; and so thank heaven for French. *Vive la France! Vive l'Empereur! Vive Bonaparte!*'

'O Rebecca, Rebecca, for shame!' cried Miss Sedley; for this was the greatest blasphemy Rebecca had as yet uttered; and in those days, in England, to say, 'Long live Bonaparte!' was as much as to say, 'Long live Lucifer!' 'How can you – how dare you have such wicked, revengeful thoughts?'

'Revenge may be wicked, but it's natural,' answered Miss Rebecca. 'I'm no angel.' And, to say the truth, she certainly was not.

Talk about

- What words in this extract do you not understand? Are these words that are now little used, have changed their meanings or are simply unfamiliar? Check the meanings in a dictionary and re-read the extract.

- Watch and discuss the opening scenes of the 1998 BBC1 television adaptation of this book.

- What do these words mean?
  direct and indirect speech
  style
  Victorian attitudes/values
  television adaptation

Closer reading

Word and sentence work

1 The narrator of all these events makes comments like 'Words refuse to tell it'; '…and actually flung…'; and '…the heroical act…'.

- What do these tell you about the narrator's tone and attitude towards what he describes?

2 How is it suggested in the first paragraph of the extract that Amelia comes from a very well-to-do family?

3 What contrasting impressions of the two Miss Pinkertons are given in the first five paragraphs of the passage?

4 How are these impressions re-inforced in the conversation about the presentation dictionary?

5 How does the structure of the last two sentences of Chapter 1 contribute to the effective ending to the chapter?

Text and genre work

6 What do we learn about Becky's character when she goes in to say goodbye to Miss Pinkerton?

7 How does Thackeray build up a sense of excitement at the impending departure of the girls?

8 Becky is given a dictionary and then throws it out of the coach window.

- How does the description of these events add to our understanding of Miss Jemima and Becky?

9 Look at Amelia's reactions when Becky throws the dictionary out of the window.

- What do these suggest about her own character?

10 At the end of the extract Becky comments, 'I'm no angel.'

- How has Thackeray built up this impression of her? Think about what Becky says and does, and the language used to describe her.

Writing practice: moving on

Think of an occasion when you 'moved on' – perhaps from one school to another, or from one house to another. Use your own memories, thoughts and feelings as the basis for a story beginning:

'Thank God I'm out of…'

Follow up!

Make a list of the 'turning points' in your life. State briefly what you felt at the time, and why they were turning points. You could do it as a table, like this:

Date	Event	Thoughts and feelings	Why it was important

- Use the material you have collected as the basis for an ongoing piece of autobiographical writing.

- If you wish to attempt something more ambitious, it could be the framework for your first novel!

Classbook reference
Unit 14, page 144